UNICORN LEADER

Driving Innovation and Influence in the Modern Workplace

Kristi Straw, MBA

Founder, Lighthouse Leadership Consultants

Contents

Introduction

Let's take it way back to where it all began for me: when I learned
to detassel corn in the sweltering summer fields of Central Illinois. Amid the endless rows of corn, my foundational lessons in
hard work and perseverance took root. Fast forward, and you'll
find me as the French Fry Girl at our local McDonald's drive-
through. It was here, between the sizzling fries and the rush of
orders, where I mastered the gift of gab and learned the art of
getting to the point quickly—skills that would later underpin my
approach to "radical candor," long before Kim Scott's incredible
book[1] made its mark on the world.

[1] Kim Scott, *Radical Candor: Fully Revised & Updated Edition: Be A Kick-Ass Boss Without Losing Your Humanity* (London: Pan Books, 2019).

These early experiences laid the groundwork for a career path that defied traditional expectations. From starting as a mortgage banker to ascending through roles such as wealth advisor, retail bank president, and finally, to the C-suite leading the wealth, retail, and call centers, my trajectory has been one of continual growth and adaptation. I have over two decades of experience transforming Fortune 500 companies through my innovative INSIGHT Method. My commitment to driving cultural transformation and fostering employee engagement has set new benchmarks in organizational development. *I have redefined the narrative for aspiring leaders by blending compassion with strategic foresight.* The culmination of this journey led me to step beyond the confines of established roles and into the ultimate leadership position as CEO of my own company.

Hi, I'm Kristi, a visionary leader and the founder of Lighthouse Leadership Consultants. *I'm a strategist by mind, rebel at heart, and unicorn in spirit.* In this new role as a CEO, I'm applying everything I have learned. Through innovative thinking, the creation of safe spaces, and an unwavering commitment to lifelong learning, our organization shows what it means to lead with resilience and determination while striving for excellence in every facet of our operation. Through my work with Lighthouse Leadership Consultants, I inspire leaders to embrace a new era of purpose-driven leadership by challenging the status quo and guiding organizations toward future-proofing their workplaces and leadership.

Enter the UNICORN Leader.

The leaders who truly leave a mark are as rare as unicorns— majestic, almost mythical, in their ability to transform visions into reality. *UNICORN Leader: Driving Innovation and Influence in the*

Modern Workplace explores embracing the loud, the quiet, the celebratory, and the reflective moments of leadership. The path of a UNICORN Leader reaches beyond adopting a new set of skills. It's about mastering skills: "you know, like nunchuck, bowhunting, and computer hacking skills."[2] While Napoleon Dynamite humorously overstates the need for eccentric skills, in the world of UNICORN Leadership, it's about undergoing a fundamental transformation that reshapes how you view and influence the world. This journey, exemplified through my experiences and innovations, and those of other leaders, demonstrates how anyone can redefine success metrics in their personal and professional lives.

Being a UNICORN Leader is about surpassing traditional roles and becoming an agent of change who navigates and thrives amid the complexities of the modern workplace. This playbook doesn't merely narrate success stories. It provides a blueprint for molding your inherent traits into powerful leadership qualities. Here, you'll discover practical strategies that can help you create a vibrant and inclusive work environment where empowered team members contribute their best.

This playbook marries the thought leadership of notable figures like Robin Speaks Jr., Vineet "Vinny" Mago, and Dr. Diedrick A. Graham (whom you will meet and learn from within these pages) along with my insights on fostering a better way to lead, where every voice—our voices—truly matter.

You will also witness the rise of a new UNICORN Leader, Gabrielle "Gabby" Rabon. She stands out as a vivid illustration of the

---

[2] *Napoleon Dynamite*, directed by Jared Hess (2004; United States: Fox Searchlight Pictures, Paramount Pictures, MTV Entertainment Studios), film.

potential within each of us. I had the privilege of mentoring Gabby and watching her metamorphosis from a conventional leader into a blossoming UNICORN Leader. Gabby's candid insights throughout this playbook offer real-world examples of how to apply these principles in various challenging environments, making the lessons both relatable and inspiring.

This playbook isn't only a guide through the complexities of modern workplaces with help from these phenomenal leaders. It's a call to action to revolutionize leadership at every turn. Armed with compassion, resilience, and a pioneering spirit, we're prepared to turn challenges into stepping stones toward a brighter future.

Consider this playbook an invitation to channel your inner UNICORN, unlock new levels of leadership potential and join a movement—**The #Stampede!**—that champions a visionary, unique, nimble-nurturing, inspired, compassionate, optimistic, resilient, and noble style of leadership. Prepare to redefine what it means to be a leader as you navigate challenges and transform them into learning moments, creating a more innovative and inclusive tomorrow.

Imagine a future where leadership links with transformative purpose, where every decision influences personal well-being, reshapes industry norms, and improves lives globally. UNICORN leadership is your gateway to **reinventing your personal brand and professional identity** and reshaping corporate America. Welcome to this call to redefine the business world—one bold, brave (and shaky) step at a time. Let's journey together, celebrating life and learning at every step because **anyone** can cultivate these traits, transforming their world and the larger world around them.

If you've ever met me, you know I'm the first to light up a room with a hearty hello or a round of applause (including jazz hands!). Yes, my voice is often the loudest: joyous and commanding space at workshops or events (sometimes it's a necessity because of venue acoustics). My vibrant exterior belies an introspective soul that deeply values vulnerability and relentlessly seeks to understand others. My journey of self-awareness, humorously akin to that meme—"Oh, you're so self-aware" and "Thanks, it's ruining my life"—is enlightening yet burdensome.

This combination of external exuberance and internal reflection embodies the essence of UNICORN Leadership. It reflects the "Nimble-Nurturing" and "Inspired" traits central to our philosophy. By openly embracing both my strengths and the challenges of self-awareness, I exemplify the holistic leadership approach that UNICORN Leaders strive for—leaders who are not only vibrant and engaging outwardly but also deeply committed to personal and communal growth inwardly. As we transition into the deeper explorations of UNICORN Leadership in the coming chapters, remember this: **true leadership involves a balance of outward influence and inward evolution.**

CHAPTER 1

The Heart and Pillars of UNICORN Leadership

The UNICORN Leader shimmers without rival. They possess a rare blend of charisma, courage, and creativity. This leader is the ENFP (Extraverted, iNtuitive, Feeling, and Perceiving)[1] of the corporate jungle—the Myers-Briggs type known for their infectious enthusiasm, boundless energy, and unshakeable belief in the potential of others. In a world that often defaults to cynicism, the UNICORN Leader stands apart for their ability to inspire and willingness to tread where others only see the mirage of impossibility.

But what makes a UNICORN Leader genuinely distinctive? Is it their penchant for seeing opportunity in adversity? Is it their

---

[1] Isabel Briggs Meyers and Peter B. Meyers, *Gifts Differing: Understanding Personality Type.* (Mountain View, California: Davies-Black Publishing,1995).

unyielding optimism in the face of daunting challenges? Is it their genuine compassion for the people they lead? The answer lies in an alchemy of all these traits and more. The heart of UNICORN leadership is the capacity to imagine a brighter future and the relentless drive to make it a reality.

By nature, the UNICORN Leader moves through life and work environments with unyielding optimism and visionary foresight. They're wired to push boundaries, envision the unseen, and forge paths where others see dead ends. A visionary UNICORN leader bears this heavy, and often misunderstood burden, with profound responsibility and undeterred commitment. In corridors where whispers of doubt and cynicism may echo, the voice of a UNICORN Leader resounds with possibility and determination.

Often misunderstood as mere dreamers, and sometimes derided or dismissed by those who cling to the same old status quo, UNICORN Leaders remain undaunted—the actual agents of change within organizations. They are the natural influencers who inspire change effortlessly, often *without formal titles or explicit recognition*. Their bravery challenges the existing corporate leadership narrative and rewrites it entirely.

For instance, consider the story of Maya, a mid-level manager in a traditional tech company, who saw potential for a new community-focused project that could both increase employee engagement and positively affect the company's brand. Despite lacking formal authority or recognition, Maya organized small, informal groups to discuss her ideas. Her enthusiasm and clear vision for a better future drew others to her, creating a movement within the company. Over time, her initiative gained momentum and what started as informal meetings became a company-endorsed project. Maya's ability to see beyond the immediate profit to focus on long-term community and employee benefits transformed the company's approach and established her as a pivotal figure in reshaping its culture.

For UNICORN Leaders like Maya, the journey of transformation isn't just a path they choose; it's an inherent call they can't ignore. This call relentlessly hunts UNICORN Leaders, driving the conviction that they're the architects of tomorrow. Their leadership style and unyielding dedication make them indispensable catalysts for change, proving that real influence often begins with a visionary willing to challenge the norm.

GABRIELLE RABON'S INSIGHT

UNICORN Leaders naturally see beyond the horizon, to see the unseen, and to plow paths where others perceive dead ends. Gabby's journey with me illuminates this trait vividly. She shared, *"Your modeling of empathy and courage showed me that I could do it too. While working on your team, I found the courage to advocate without fear, showcasing the power of empathetic, bold leadership."*

Gabby's experience is a testament to the UNICORN Leader's ability to inspire their team to navigate challenges and transform them into opportunities for reflection, growth, and creativity. Remember, the essence of being a UNICORN Leader lies not in belonging to a rare Myers-Briggs personality type or being extroverted, but in the courage to be distinct, intentional, able to lead with empathy and challenge the status quo with a blend of creativity and strategic insight.

DEFINING UNICORN LEADER TRAITS

A distinct set of attributes, each represented by a letter in UNICORN, characterizes a UNICORN Leader. These traits define the approach of these leaders and underscore their effectiveness in fostering environments where creativity, empathy, and resilience thrive.

UNIQUE

Authenticity, and the courage to stand out, distinguishes UNICORN Leaders from everyone else. For example, Sherri, a startup founder, implemented a radical flat management structure that encouraged all employees to contribute ideas, generating a hotbed of innovation and making her company a standout in a competitive industry.

NIMBLE-NURTURING

These leaders expertly balance rapid responsiveness with deep care for their team's development and well-being. Consider Alex, who quickly shifted his team to remote work at the start of a crisis, ensuring that each team member could access professional development workshops. As a result, his team maintained morale and productivity.

INSPIRING

Through their integrity and visionary leadership, UNICORN Leaders motivate their teams. Sarah, a nonprofit director, shared her vision for global impact through community programs, inspiring her team to double their efforts, and significantly expanded the organization's reach.

COMPASSIONATE

UNICORN Leaders lead with empathy and model desired behaviors. Jordan, a hospital administrator, regularly schedules time to walk through departments, engaging with staff and patients to foster a culture of care and commitment that translates into high patient satisfaction scores.

OPTIMISTIC

By maintaining a positive outlook, UNICORN Leaders instill hope and confidence in their teams. Maria faced significant budget cuts, but she framed the challenge as an opportunity to streamline and innovate. She led her team to develop cost-effective solutions that improved service delivery.

RESILIENT

These leaders are adept at bouncing back from setbacks. After a failed product launch, Tarik used the experience as a teaching moment, encouraging his team to analyze the failure without blame and to come back stronger with a successful redesign.

NOBLE

UNICORN Leaders are driven by a deeply rooted purpose that eclipses personal gain or fame. For instance, Addie, a tech CEO, redirected substantial company profits into local community education programs, aiming to build a knowledgeable future workforce that benefits society at large.

WHY BEING A UNICORN LEADER MAKES YOU UNSTOPPABLE

How can a leader not only adapt but thrive amid the chaos of global business? Say hello to the prowess of a UNICORN Leader, who transcends typical leadership roles and positions as change agents, unstoppable in any industry. Distinguished by their unique blend of empathy, resilience, and visionary insight, these leaders spearhead change and craft the future with a bold and strategic approach.

When I took charge of a large retail banking division, I started with minimal experience in that sector. What I carried with me was a fresh perspective anchored in the principles of UNICORN leadership. From Day One, my mission was to infuse the organizational culture with transparency, kindness, and a drive for learning that was unprecedented in that banking environment.

The division I inherited languished beneath the weight of low employee engagement and uninspiring sales figures. A transformative approach was needed—not just in operations, but in how team members felt about their work. I introduced regular, dynamic training sessions that surpassed enhancing skills. The training empowered employees to take initiative and innovate, to view themselves as integral drivers of our division's success.

Within months, the impact of these changes became clear. Employee engagement metrics, previously dismal, soared and exceeded the industry average, setting a new benchmark within our organization. More impressively, this renewed vigor translated directly to our sales performance. By the end of my first year, we had nearly doubled the sales figures achieved by my more seasoned peers.

Grassroots efforts kept our approach to innovation grounded. We advocated ideas from all levels of the team, cultivating a sense of ownership and collaboration across the division. This led to the development and launch of several new product lines. Crafted from direct employee feedback and a keen understanding of customer needs, these products addressed gaps that traditional banking offerings missed. Their success was overwhelming throughout the division, which included Georgia, North Carolina, and parts of Florida. Soon, HQ rolled out the product lines throughout the bank, revolutionizing our customer engagement and service delivery.

Integral to our division's success was the creation of a psychologically safe workplace—an environment where people felt valued and free to experiment and learn from mistakes. This wasn't just about avoiding errors; it was about leveraging them as a spring-board for growth and innovation. Our division transformed into a vibrant hub for banking innovation, influencing company-wide standards and practices.

And, in this spirit of transformation, we launched a volunteer marketing campaign that symbolized our new ethos. We infused our values of kindness and empathy into every facet of the organization, culminating in a campaign that featured T-shirts, hashtags, and hats, all adorned with an actual heart integrated into the brand name. This campaign, which I led, bolstered our brand identity and left a lasting imprint on the company's culture. To this day, the brand remains a vibrant symbol of the commitment to lead with heart.

UNICORN leadership traits—driven by empathy, resilience, and visionary thinking—can dramatically shift organizational dynamics. By prioritizing clarity, kindness, and continuous skill development, we didn't just meet our targets; we created a thriving workplace culture that fostered massive growth and experimentation, leading to exceptional results in both employee satisfaction and business outcomes. And through it all, we infused kindness and empathy into every corner of the organization.

GABRIELLE RABON'S INSIGHT

"Being under your leadership, I have allowed myself to be more bold, to take more risks and not be afraid to voice what's on my mind, which really gave me a platform to be more effective as a leader," reflects Gabby. Her journey underlines the unstoppable nature of a UNICORN Leader, showcasing how the nurturing and empowering environment we cultivated led her to thrive in scenarios where previously she might have hesitated.

Empirical data supports the unmatched effectiveness (and adoration) of leaders who embody UNICORN traits. Organizations under their guidance achieve higher innovation rates and enjoy enhanced workplace harmony and productivity. High levels of psychological safety, a direct result of empathetic leadership, correlate strongly with organizational success and market leadership.

HALLMARK EXAMPLES OF UNICORN LEADERS

The hallmarks of a UNICORN Leader—Unique, Nurturing, Inspiring, Compassionate, Optimistic, Resilient, and Noble—emerge as foundational pillars that propel their influence and triumph across most industries. Allow me to introduce you to three exemplary individuals whose careers embody the UNICORN ethos. You'll learn from them in the pages to come.

Each leader adapts UNICORN principles across diverse sectors, spanning finance to healthcare to strategic consulting. Delve into the wisdom of Robin, Vinny, and Dr. Graham to unearth the transformative power and adaptability of UNICORN traits, illustrating how authentic, visionary leadership transcends conventional boundaries.

ROBIN SPEAKS JR.: A BEACON OF NOBLE AND RESILIENT LEADERSHIP

Robin Speaks Jr. has robust experience in the banking sector and embodies the Noble and Resilient traits of UNICORN leadership. In an industry where high pressures and compassion might be underestimated,[2] Robin consistently shows that integrity and resilience can drive significant organizational success and create a respectful work environment.

- **Noble:** Robin is renowned for his unwavering ethical standards and transparency, inspiring his team to uphold these values vigorously.

- **Resilient:** Robin's resilience has enabled him and his team to view challenges as opportunities for growth and development in the face of financial sector volatility.

[2] J. Smith, "The Role of Compassion in High-Pressure Industries," *Harvard Business Review*, January 2020, https://hbr.org/2020/01/the-role-of-compassion-in-high-pressure-industries.

VINEET 'VINNY' MAGO: MASTER OF OPTIMISTIC AND INNOVATIVE LEADERSHIP

Vinny Mago's journey is a testament to turning personal challenges into professional successes. He applies his Optimistic and Innovative traits to inspire and enact change within the healthcare and financial services industries.

- **Optimistic:** Vinny's enduring optimism boosts his team's morale, fostering a can-do spirit that turns potential setbacks into opportunities.

- **Innovative:** At the cutting-edge of technology and ideas, Vinny cultivates a workplace that encourages and expects innovation, which propels his team to industry leadership.

DR. DIEDRICK A. GRAHAM: CHAMPION OF COMPASSION AND NIMBLE-NURTURING

Dr. Diedrick A. Graham exemplifies Compassionate and Nimble-Nurturing leadership traits in consulting, focusing on the cultural and strategic dimensions that enhance organizational dynamics and morale.

- **Compassionate:** He anchors his leadership in profound empathy for his team, which creates an inclusive atmosphere where all feel valued.

- **Nimble-Nurturing:** Dr. Graham excels in creating an agile and supportive workplace, skillfully balancing rapid adaptability with a deep commitment to his team's personal and professional growth. This approach cultivates a workplace where individuals and the collective thrive, seamlessly blending responsiveness with empowerment.

ACTIONABLE STRATEGIES FOR UNICORN LEADERS:

By embracing and integrating the strategies identified in this section, UNICORN Leaders excel and drive profound, lasting effects within their organizations and industries. They create environments where teams feel safe to explore, innovate, and grow, making the concept of being unstoppable a reality.

Foster Continuous Learning

Start a book club focused on leadership and innovation within your organization. This will encourage continuous professional development and nurture a culture rooted in shared knowledge and mutual growth. Start with Brené Brown's *Dare to Lead: Brave Work. Tough Conversations.* Whole Hearts.,[3] a pivotal resource that delves into the courage and vulnerability necessary for transformative leadership.

---

[3] Brené Brown, *Dare to Lead: Brave Work. Tough Conversations.* Whole Hearts (New York: Random House, 2018).

Cultivate Meaningful Engagement

Schedule regular one-on-one meetings to foster a healthier work environment. Transform these sessions into opportunities for growth by incorporating structured feedback using three pivotal questions:

- What am I doing well?
- What should I stop doing?
- What am I not doing that you would like me to do?

These questions show your commitment to adapting to your team's needs, reflecting a core UNICORN principle of responsive leadership.

GABRIELLE RABON'S INSIGHT

"These one-on-one sessions transformed how I saw my role and responsibilities. The structured feedback not only refined my skills but also solidified my confidence in leading with vision and compassion," Gabby adds. Her experience exemplifies how responsive leadership can empower team members to excel beyond their limits.

Encourage Open Communication

Supplement one-on-one meetings with regular forums where team members share ideas and feedback without fear of reprisal. Building a culture of open communication enhances trust and supports a nurturing workplace ripe for innovation and problem-solving.

Celebrate Failures as Learning Opportunities
Establish a "fail-forward" culture where your team views mistakes as essential steps toward mastery and innovation. Highlight and celebrate these learning moments to demystify failure and promote a culture of risk-taking and continuous improvement.

GABRIELLE RABON'S INSIGHT

Reflecting on the start of her UNICORN Leader journey, Gabby shares, *"Under Kristi's mentorship, I was encouraged to embrace skills beyond the conventional—nurturing not just technical abilities but also emotional intelligence and visionary thinking. This holistic development reshaped my understanding of what effective leadership looks like in action."*

As we integrate these stories and strategies, the unique leadership styles of luminary UNICORN Leaders like Robin, Vinny, and Dr. Graham, along with Gabrielle's direct application of these principles, demonstrate the powerful impact of UNICORN leadership traits. Together, they have not only achieved remarkable professional success but have also fostered work environments characterized by innovation, empathy, and resilience. Gabrielle's insights, and the collective experiences of these leaders, bring to life the sometimes abstract or even "squishy" traits of UNICORN leadership. They offer practical steps that any leader can take to create a more compassionate and joyful workplace.

Gabrielle Rabon's Quick Tips for Embodying UNICORN Traits
Gabby shares straightforward advice based on her own experiences as a leader. With these simple, yet powerful actions you can strengthen your leadership, bit by bit, every day.

1. **Unique:**
   - **Tip:** *"Lean into what makes you different. Use your unique superpowers to leave a memorable mark in your leadership role."*

2. **Nimble-Nurturing:**
   - **Tip:** *"Make time to talk with your team about more than just work. Show interest in their career and personal development and create space for them to share about their hobbies, interests, etc. outside of work, if they're comfortable doing so. And, when their interests or pursuits change or evolve, grow with them and adapt your leadership to their needs in any given phase of their personal OR professional development."*

3. **Inspiring:**
   - **Tip:** *"Tell your team about times you've faced messy situations and come through. It'll show them that challenges are just a few extra steps to climb before reaching success."*

4. Compassionate:

- **Tip:** *"Always start by putting yourself in your team's shoes. Understanding their struggles by asking genuinely curious questions will help you support them better."*

5. Optimistic:

- **Tip:** *"Keep a positive attitude, even when things go wrong. Don't shy away from sharing the challenges that are appropriate. This is a great opportunity for team problem solving and deepening their trust in your leadership. Your team will pick up on your vibe and stay motivated."*

6. Resilient:

- **Tip:** *"Show your team how to learn from mistakes instead of fearing them."*

7. Noble:

- **Tip:** "Be honest and open, always. Trust is built when you're clear about the good and the bad."

Gabby's tips offer practical steps you can use right now to boost your leadership style. They're drawn from real life, designed to make a noticeable difference in how you lead, beginning now.

CHAPTER 2

Mastering Compassion and Nimble-Nurturing

How often do you feel truly understood by your leaders? Do you experience a sense of genuine support in your workplace? Can the warmth of compassion transform an office into a sanctuary of growth and innovation? In the leadership landscape, where many qualities merge to shape the ideal leader's profile, the subtle yet influential attributes of Compassion and Nimble-Nurturing often remain overshadowed. These traits, akin to the comforting warmth of sunlight after a storm, provide essential reassurance and warmth, vital elements for transforming work environments into havens of growth and positivity.

In this section, we dig into the remarkable influence of Dr. Diedrick A. Graham, a UNICORN Leader whose compassionate and nimble-nurturing leadership style exemplifies the transformative power of these qualities. My experience with Dr. Graham's mentorship for over five years has provided me with a firsthand look at how his leadership style can deeply reshape professional environments. His guidance revolutionized my approach, instilling a commitment to foster a workplace where every individual feels valued and equipped for growth.

One pivotal lesson from Dr. Graham that deeply influenced my leadership during a critical period of sales process and accountability reforms at a $30 billion-dollar bank was the principle that "change can only happen at the speed of trust." This insight was crucial as it guided me through complex transformations by emphasizing the need to build and maintain trust with the team. With Dr. Graham's advice, I focused on nurturing trust through transparency, consistent communication, and genuine responsiveness to the team's concerns and suggestions.

For example, while leading these sweeping changes, I started a series of trust-building workshops inspired by Dr. Graham's methodologies. The workshops removed barriers within the team and cultivated a more collaborative environment. As trust grew, so did the team's willingness to embrace new processes, which significantly enhanced our overall efficiency and sales outcomes.

Dr. Graham's insights were also instrumental during periods of significant organizational change, providing strategies for maintaining transparency and trust. By adopting his approach, I guided my team through a major restructuring with minimal resistance, which increased the commitment from all stakeholders.

The leadership principles developed by Dr. Graham are deeply actionable and resonate with the core messages of this chapter. His enduring impact on my career exemplifies the profound effect that leading with empathy, with a focus on nurturing potential, can have on both individuals and organizations.

DR. GRAHAM'S PERSONAL STORY

Dr. Graham often reflects on a critical moment that reshaped his approach to leadership, illustrating his commitment to compassionate and nurturing principles. Inspired by this Dr. Martin Luther King, Jr. quote, *"Our goal is to create a beloved community, and this will require a qualitative change in our souls as well as a quantitative change in our lives,"*[1] Dr. Graham shares an incident where he applied these principles during a challenging project:

"I once led a team facing significant project delays, which caused immense stress. Recognizing the strain on my team, I arranged for a series of workshops on stress management, personal growth, and resilience. This initiative didn't focus on getting the project back on track, but on ensuring the team felt supported and valued. The result? We met our deadlines, and the team felt more cohesive and motivated than ever."

[1] The King Philosophy – Nonviolence365®, The King Center, March 26, 2024, https://tinyurl.com/u7stkvzt

COMPASSIONATE LEADERSHIP IN ACTION

Empathy toward team members, understanding their unique circumstances, and responding with genuine care and support characterizes compassionate leadership. Dr. Graham's leadership approach showcases how compassion extends beyond empathy to create tangible changes in workplace culture.

- **Empathy and Understanding:** Dr. Graham emphasizes the importance of genuinely understanding the personal and professional challenges of team members. By acknowledging these challenges, he promotes a culture of trust and openness.

- **Supportive Communication:** Using Nonviolent Communication (NVC),[2] Dr. Graham engages in dialogues, prioritizing clear, empathetic, and supportive communication. This method ensures all team members feel heard and valued, enhancing their engagement and productivity.

NIMBLE-NURTURING LEADERSHIP IN PRACTICE

Nurturing involves more than professional development. It encompasses a holistic growth environment where team members develop their strengths and address their weaknesses in a supportive setting. By adopting a nimble-nurturing approach, leaders further encourage

[2] Marshall B. Rosenberg, *Nonviolent Communication: A Language of Life* (Encinitas, CA: PuddleDancer Press, 2003), pp. 220.

an agile culture, enabling them to swiftly adapt to the needs and aspirations of their team. This next-level ability ensures that support is both consistent and responsive, and effectively aligned with the changing personal and professional needs of team members.

- **Fostering Development:** Dr. Graham creates opportunities to grow through challenging training programs and mentorship opportunities that stretch team members' capabilities.

- **Encouraging Potential:** Dr. Graham boosts their confidence by recognizing and promoting each team member's potential, which prepares them to advance a more dynamic and capable team.

ADVICE FOR ASPIRING LEADERS FROM DR. GRAHAM

Dr. Graham, a beacon of compassionate leadership, offers invaluable guidance for those looking to refine their leadership approach. Here's how you can incorporate his teachings into your leadership style:

1. **Embrace Nonviolent Communication (NVC):**
   - Dr. Graham advises: "For leaders eager to enhance their compassionate leadership skills, I recommend wholeheartedly embracing the principles of Nonviolent Communication (NVC) as both a daily practice and a way of being."

- **Actionable Strategy:** Begin by integrating NVC into your daily interactions. Focus on openly expressing your feelings and needs and inviting your team to do the same. This fosters a collaborative environment where team members approach conflicts with curiosity and a desire to understand, rather than with defensiveness.

2. **Cultivate Self-Awareness and Vulnerability:**
   - **Dr. Graham notes:** "Adopting this compassionate approach requires considerable courage, self-awareness, and vulnerability—qualities that may initially feel uncomfortable because of traditional leadership models that equate strength with toughness."
   - **Actionable Strategy:** Schedule regular self-reflection sessions. Use reflective journaling or mindfulness exercises to explore your feelings, biases, and reactions. This introspection can improve your understanding of your team's dynamics and enhance your empathetic responses.

3. **Develop a Routine for Continuous Emotional Growth:**
   - **Dr. Graham suggests:** "The journey towards compassionate leadership is ongoing and requires continuous self-reflection and growth. Techniques like mindfulness, self-empathy, and reflective journaling can be invaluable."
   - **Actionable Strategy:** Implement mindfulness practices both personally and within your team. For example, start meetings with a one-minute meditation or provide

resources for emotional resilience training to help everyone become more present and engaged.

4. **Prioritize Human Needs Equally with Business Tasks:**
   - **Dr. Graham explains:** "As we become more present and attentive, we can better listen to and understand our teams' needs and feelings while also remaining flexible in our approach. We foster an environment where human needs are just as important as the tasks."
   - **Actionable Strategy:** Adopt a "human-first" approach in project management and daily tasks. Encourage your team to share personal insights and challenges in regular meetings, ensuring these aspects are valued and addressed alongside business objectives.

THE IMPACT OF COMPASSIONATE AND NIMBLE-NURTURING LEADERSHIP

Studies by organizations such as Gallup have shown that employees who feel their supervisors are empathetic and supportive are significantly more engaged. Research in organizational psychology shows that nurturing environments contribute to higher job satisfaction and better overall employee mental health. These sources support more compassionate and nurturing work environments. The benefits of implementing compassionate and nurturing leadership are widespread and include (but are not limited to):

- **Enhanced Team Cohesion.** Teams led by compassionate and nurturing leaders exhibit stronger bonds, translating to improved collaboration and efficiency.

- **Increased Employee Satisfaction and Retention.** Compassionate and nurturing workplaces attract and keep talent, reducing turnover and building a more experienced and committed workforce.

- **Higher Productivity and Innovation.** Teams that feel supported are more likely to take creative risks, leading to higher levels of innovation.

Through the lens of Dr. Graham's leadership, Compassion and Nimble-Nurturing are beneficial and essential UNICORN traits for modern leadership. These traits cultivate a workspace that meets employees' needs and prepares them to meet future challenges with resilience and enthusiasm.

A NOTABLE NUGGET
FROM GABRIELLE RABON

"Leadership before I met you was pretty tradi- tional. It was still pretty much—lots of times— they 'talked the talk', but that was it," Gabby says. "They talked about being this servant leader, open to new ideas and new ways of driving culture and impact. But in reality, that wasn't the case, and sometimes when their leadership or their deci- sion-making was challenged, that was frowned upon, and I almost always feared retaliation."

Gabby's experience and reflection underscore the urgent need for today's leaders to create an environment that encourages and celebrates open communication. By moving away from fear-based management, we can cultivate a culture that truly values innovation and honest feedback.

CHAPTER 3

Noble Leadership and Resilience

Everyone knows that business is all about quick wins, right? Wrong. Against the ever-evolving business landscape, where short-term gains often overshadow long-term principles, Robin Speaks Jr. stands out as a beacon of noble and resilient leadership. His illustrious career in the banking industry demonstrates how a steadfast commitment to integrity and resilience can lead to sustainable success and inspire a culture of trust and loyalty.

Having worked closely with Robin, I had a front-row seat to his remarkable integrity and resilience. His leadership not only elevated our organization but also influenced my ever-evolving approach to leadership. Despite facing unjust accusations and unfair treatment from those who appeared to be allies, Robin continued to lead with compassion and unwavering nobility.

This difficult time magnified the essence of leadership, which is often tested not during easy times, but amid adversity. Robin's response to obstacles was anything but passive; he actively upheld his principles, demonstrating that a UNICORN Leader does not succumb to pressures or threats. Instead, he continued to embody the values of compassion and integrity, reinforcing the fact that authentic leadership is about standing firm in one's values, even in the face of opposition. Robin's steadfastness during these trials has shaped my perspective on leadership and highlighted the powerful impact of leading with authenticity and ethical courage.

NOBLE LEADERSHIP IN PRACTICE

A profound commitment to ethics, transparency, and fairness characterizes nobility in leadership. Robin's approach to leadership is born from these principles and embodies a model that merges resilience with a solid moral compass. This leadership combination steers companies through turbulent times and builds trust and respect among all stakeholders.

- **Ethical Decision-Making:** During a stringent salary and budget planning phase, senior management urged Robin to adjust performance review scores to align more closely with budget constraints, which would have resulted in unfairly lowered salaries for specific team members. Recognizing the ethical implications and potential unfairness, Robin instead audited existing salaries within his team. The comprehensive review revealed broader discrepancies and inequities that had gone unnoticed. By addressing these issues head-on, Robin ensured fair salary adjustments, a management step that reinforced his commitment to integrity and equitable treatment for every employee. Ultimately, this leadership approach strengthened trust and respect within the team.

- **Transparency in Communication:** Robin's commitment to transparency was crucial during a period of rapid change. Senior management adjusted goals and metrics for roles within the banking center in a brief span. Understanding the potential confusion and frustration this could cause, Robin managed the situation flawlessly by holding a series of educational sessions for all employees. In these sessions, he clearly outlined the reasons behind the changes, the expected benefits, and how these adjustments would align with broader company objectives. He also organized an open forum for employees to ask questions and express concerns. This approach educated the team and maintained morale and engagement during the transition process.

RESILIENCE THROUGH CHALLENGES

Resilience includes bouncing back from setbacks, but it also means using challenges as stairways to more significant achievements. Robin's career offers several vital moments where his resilience shone brightly:

- **Overcoming Adversity:** As the pandemic unfolded, the banking industry faced unprecedented challenges, particularly for branches that couldn't transition to remote work. Circumstances thrust Robin's team into a whirlwind of adaptability. Usual operations faced a swift pivot when they had to conduct all transactions through drive-through windows. With no precedent for this level of disruption, Robin led his team with exemplary agility.

He quickly implemented changes to existing policies to accommodate the new operational demands and arranged for his team to work in shifts that allowed them to manage their workload effectively while maintaining safety. His leadership was crucial in training the team to handle tense interactions gracefully as they navigated educating customers on new safety protocols, including mask-wearing, amid a backdrop of political tension and public frustration.

Robin's open communication and constant availability helped ease the team's anxiety during trying times. He held daily briefings to update policies as the situation changed and created a feedback loop that allowed team members to voice their concerns and suggest improvements in real-time. This approach kept operations running smoothly. The team felt supported and valued, and they found a sense of unity and purpose despite the chaos.

Under Robin's leadership, the bank functioned with a level of service that maintained and even enhanced customer trust and loyalty. His ability to lead through adversity with calmness, adaptability, and foresight exemplified noble and resilient leadership traits in action. Robin led his team through the storm with a steady hand and a clear vision.

- **Continuous Improvement:** Robin's belief that every challenge is a springboard for growth truly comes to life in his approach to improving the banking center environment. After a significant project initially fell short of its goals, Robin saw an opportunity not just for recovery, but for transformation. Rather than pointing fingers or succumbing to discouragement, he organized a series of creative and engaging workshops that emphasized learning from the experience.

In these workshops, which quickly became a highlight of the team's routine, Robin encouraged everyone to discuss openly what went wrong and brainstorm innovative solutions. These sessions became creative labs where fun and experimentation flourished. For instance, one workshop used role-playing games to simulate customer interactions based on the recent project's challenges, allowing team members to think on their feet and inject humor into their problem-solving processes.

This shift toward a more dynamic and enjoyable work environment helped to rectify the issues from the failed project and elevated a culture of continuous improvement. Every setback became a chance to innovate and improve. This enhanced day-to-day operations and significantly boosted morale and team cohesion.

Through these initiatives, Robin effectively transformed potential negatives into opportunities for growth and creativity, making the banking center a more vibrant and enjoyable place to work. His leadership generated substantial improvements in project outcomes and operational efficiencies and caused the daily work experience to become more fulfilling for every team member.

The impact of Robin's leadership style extends beyond the immediate successes of his team and projects. His commitment to nobility and resilience has cultivated a workplace environment where employees feel valued and understood, leading to high retention rates and deep loyalty within his team. In the underappreciated landscape of leadership, nobility and resilience may not grab headlines, but they are the unsung heroes that forge legacies of lasting influence and integrity.

Through his example, Robin has not only advanced his career but has inspired a new generation of leaders who emulate his values of integrity and resilience against a business landscape dominated by the desire for quick wins. Robin Speaks Jr. emerges as a paragon of Noble and Resilient UNICORN leadership. His storied career in the banking industry, adorned with both formidable challenges and substantial triumphs, shows the power of steadfast dedication to integrity and resilience—a commitment that encourages sustainable success and cultivates a culture of trust and loyalty.

Working closely with Robin, I've had the privilege of witnessing his remarkable integrity and resilience up close. His leadership approach has shaped our organization tremendously, lifting us to new heights and influencing my evolving leadership perspective. Robin's active defense of his principles during these turbulent times showed the core of UNICORN leadership. It's about not bending to pressures or threats but embodying the values of compassion and integrity consistently. This resolve during trials has influenced my perspective on leadership and highlighted the potent effect of leading authentically and with ethical courage.

NOBLE LEADERSHIP IN PRACTICE

Robin's leadership style, characterized by a deep commitment to ethics, transparency, and fairness, serves as a lighthouse for guiding companies through challenging times while building trust and respect among all stakeholders. His consistent and ethical decision-making, even when presented with easier, less honorable paths, has garnered immense respect from peers and subordinates alike. Moreover, Robin's commitment to maintaining open lines of communication ensures that decisions are transparent and understood throughout the organization in an inclusive atmosphere.

RESILIENCE THROUGH CHALLENGES

Resilience under Robin's leadership extends beyond merely bouncing back from setbacks; it involves leveraging challenges as catalysts for greater achievements. For instance, during the financial crisis, Robin's calm and composed leadership guided his team through uncertainty, and his optimism reassured them, enabling a successful journey through the 2008 housing crisis. He views each challenge as a growth opportunity, constantly encouraging his team to learn from each experience and promoting an environment where continuous improvement is the norm.

The influence of Robin's leadership extends beyond immediate team successes. His commitment to noble principles and resilient conduct has fostered a workplace where employees feel genuinely valued and understood, resulting in high retention rates and deep loyalty. This environment, often underappreciated in leadership discussions, showcases how nobility and resilience might not always capture headlines but are extremely meaningful in forging legacies of lasting influence and integrity.

ADVICE AND IMPACT

Drawing from Robin's example, here are actionable strategies for leaders aspiring to incorporate nobility and resilience into their leadership style:

- **Ethical Decision-Making:** Prioritize what is right over what is easy. This practice builds trust and sets a moral standard for your team.

- **Transparency in Communication:** Keep your team informed about decisions and the rationale behind them to foster an atmosphere of trust and inclusivity.

- **Using Challenges as Growth Opportunities:** Encourage your team to view setbacks as chances to learn and grow. This establishes a culture that values resilience and adaptability.

Robin's insights serve as this chapter's cornerstone for leaders who aspire to Robin's achievement level when adopting the UNICORN leadership traits of Nobility and Resilience. His leadership not only propels his own career forward, but it inspires a new generation of leaders to embrace and champion these values.

REVISITING GABRIELLE RABON'S TRANSFORMATIVE LEADERSHIP EXPERIENCE

Earlier, we introduced Gabrielle Rabon, whose experiences under transformative leadership exemplify the significant impact guidance can have on an individual's personal and professional growth. Her journey provides a compelling testament to the power of resilient leadership:

**A NOTABLE NUGGET
FROM GABRIELLE RABON**

*"Just from being under your leadership, The UNI-CORN Leader Way, **I have allowed myself to be more bold, take more risks, swallow my fears and voice what's on my mind.** After all these years of leadership, I found my voice working under you."*

Gabby's testimonial vividly illustrates how noble and resilient leadership not only supports but actively cultivates the personal development of its followers. Through her experience, we see how leadership, when committed to ethical principles and resilience, can transform apprehension into assertiveness, encouraging team members to embrace challenges with a fresh perspective.

CHAPTER 4

Harnessing Optimism and Innovation

How does leadership grow in a world of relentless technological change and intense global competition? No area remains unaffected by these shifts—they reach into every corner of our connected globe. Vineet "Vinny" Mago showcases the critical traits of optimism and innovation in leadership, expertly guiding his teams through these challenges. This chapter examines how Vinny's strategic vision creates fertile ground for breakthroughs and fortifies resilience and adaptability among his team members.

Vinny often shares stories from his career to illustrate the power of innovative thinking. One such story takes place when he led a project that faltered because of outdated practices:

"In the face of declining performance on a high-priority project, rather than revert to traditional tactics that were clearly not yielding the desired results, I chose a different leadership approach. I gathered the team for a special brainstorming session, explicitly encouraging them to think without constraints—a 'sky's the limit' mentality that was somewhat unconventional within our usual operational framework.

"To facilitate this creative process, we used various innovative brainstorming techniques, such as 'reverse thinking' and 'role storming,' to challenge our usual perspectives and ignite new ideas. Each team member, regardless of their traditional role, was asked to contribute as if they were the project leader, providing fresh insights and proposing solutions from unique vantage points.

"The result was a revolutionary approach that not only saved the project but also set a new industry standard. We developed a new software tool that automated a significant portion of our data analysis, dramatically reducing the time and resources previously required. This tool not only expedited our project timeline but also enhanced the accuracy and reliability of our data, leading to more informed decision-making."

As shown several times so far in this playbook, an environment founded on proactive risk-taking, along with the safe space to make mistakes, promotes an environment rich in creativity, joy, and purpose!

OPTIMISTIC LEADERSHIP IN ACTION

Optimism in leadership extends far beyond mere positive thinking. It involves a proactive approach to viewing challenges as opportunities and instilling hope and motivation within teams. Vinny's leadership style validates how optimism effectively drives an organization's strategy and growth.

- **Inspiring Confidence:** Vinny's vibrant energy and unwavering optimism act as a catalyst that ignites his team's enthusiasm for ambitious projects. During the launch of a challenging initiative to integrate advanced technology into existing systems, Vinny's confidence in his team's capabilities played a critical role. At the project kickoff, he not only shared compelling stories of past successes that were initially deemed high-risk, but he also radiated a contagious energy that lifted everyone's spirits. He highlighted the individual strengths of team members, reinforcing his genuine belief in their ability to succeed. This energy motivated the team to engage with the project with both skill and passion. They shared a collective belief in their inevitable success.

- **Maintaining Morale:** Vinny's ability to maintain high team morale, even during setbacks, further showcases his positive leadership style and dynamic energy. When a key project encountered unexpected regulatory hurdles, causing significant delays, Vinny's response was exemplary. Instead of dwelling on the setbacks, he organized a team gathering that celebrated current progress and reassessed planned strategies. His vibrant energy during this event transformed potential discouragement into renewed motivation. Vinny consistently uses his high-energy leadership, indicative of a high-performing leader on the Energy Leadership Index,[1] to transform challenges into motivational stepping stones. His positive demeanor, and the energy he brings to every interaction, reassures the team to view obstacles as temporary and surmountable, and helps maintain a culture where resilience and optimism activate success.

INFLUENCING WITH OPTIMISM: IMPACT ON ORGANIZATIONAL CULTURE AND PERFORMANCE

As we prepared for our work on this project, Vinny shared the importance of regularly assessing team engagement and morale. He emphasizes that this practice is significant for leaders. "While I could easily recite numerous statistics from my career demonstrating the positive impacts of optimistic leadership on business metrics such as performance, engagement, retention, and profitability, it might be more beneficial to focus on practical indicators," he suggests.

This approach helps leaders continuously gauge the "temperature" of their teams. Below are several key indicators Vinny recommends leaders must watch for in their team members—and in themselves—to assess the influence of optimism in leadership. By closely monitoring these indicators, leaders can confirm the outcomes of their optimistic approach and its broad impact on organizational culture and performance. This conversation with Vinny was so enlightening that it inspired the inclusion of this checklist

---

[1] Bruce D. Schneider, *Energy Leadership: The 7 Level Framework for Mastery in Life and Business*, (Hoboken, N.J.: John Wiley & Sons, Inc., 2022).

in our playbook, providing valuable insights for leaders seeking to develop a positive and productive workplace:

- **Employee Well-Being:** Are team members appearing happier and less stressed?

- **Creativity and Innovation:** Has there been a noticeable improvement in the team's creativity?

- **Communication Enhancement:** Are conversations more frequent between teammates who previously interacted minimally? Are these discussions crossing team boundaries?

- **Engagement and Referrals:** Are team members actively referring others for open positions within the department?

- **Expertise Sharing:** Is there an uptick in team members volunteering their knowledge and solutions?

- **Cross-Management Interaction:** Are other managers increasingly seeking to collaborate with your team?

- **Inclusion in Strategic Decisions:** Have you been included in meetings or projects previously outside your involvement?

- **Mentorship and Leadership:** Are individuals seeking guidance and mentorship from you or your team members?

- **Ownership and Passion:** Are team members taking ownership of their work and showing more extraordinary passion?

- **Cultural Shifts:** Have typically outspoken or negative team members become more accepting and supportive?

- **Supportive Environment:** Is proactive support being offered and accepted within the team?

- **Resilience in Adversity:** Does the team collectively display resilience when challenges arise?

INSPIRING INNOVATION

Under Vinny's leadership, innovation requires more than sporadic breakthroughs, but it involves a consistent effort to grow and enhance every aspect of operations. This continuous push for innovation directly aligns with the Inspiring aspect of the UNICORN Leader framework, where leaders not only motivate their teams toward achieving common goals but also foster a community ripe for creativity and forward-thinking.

- **Encouraging Experimentation:** Vinny champions a culture that encourages and celebrates calculated risks as essential elements of the learning process. He understands that true innovation stems from the willingness to venture into the unknown and experiment. By treating failures as valuable learning opportunities, Vinny inspires his team to push boundaries and innovate without fear. This approach resonates deeply with the Inspiring facet of the UNICORN framework, as it motivates team members to embrace challenges and transform potential setbacks into stepping stones for success.

- **Leveraging Technology:** Always on the cutting edge, Vinny ensures that his team and company remain at the forefront of industry innovation by integrating the latest technologies seamlessly. This streamlines processes and significantly enhances productivity. As a result, team members stay ahead of market trends and technological advancements. By harnessing such tools, Vinny not only optimizes operational efficiency but inspires his team by demonstrating how to leverage technology to achieve superior results. This strategic use of technology underpins the inspiring component of leadership and showcases how visionary thinking and innovative tools lead to substantial improvements and new industry standards.

THE IMPACT OF OPTIMISM AND INNOVATION

Research shows that leaders who embrace and drive innovation create environments with up to 30 percent higher employee satisfaction rates and significantly more excellent financial performance. A separate study on leadership reveals that optimistic leaders achieve higher team cohesion and resilience, directly affecting productivity and retention. The combination of optimism and innovation in leadership can result in:

- **Driving Growth:** Optimistic and innovative leaders like Vinny can drive sustainable growth by constantly seeking and implementing new ideas.

- **Enhancing Adaptability:** These traits keep organizations accountable so that they adapt to market changes or technology more effectively.

- **Fostering Team Spirit:** Teams led by optimistic and innovative leaders are more engaged, committed, and satisfied with their work. They also have more fun!

Vinny Mago's use of the UNICORN leadership traits of Optimism and Inspiration exemplifies how these attributes transform leadership effectiveness. This chapter highlights Vinny's achievements and provides actionable insights to develop these qualities in your leadership style. Through his story, we learn that a positive outlook, combined with a creative approach to problem-solving, propels organizations forward and undergirds them with a culture of resilience and adaptability. Leaders who embody these characteristics inspire their teams to explore new ideas, push boundaries, and achieve collective success. Vinny's leadership philosophy shows the power of facing the future with optimism and ingenuity.

CHAPTER 5

Nurturing a UNICORN Culture

Anchoring every organizational layer in the foundational values of UNICORN leadership plays a major role in nurturing a vibrant UNICORN culture, where leaders vigorously support the principles of uniqueness, empathy, and resilience. Integral to this approach is active listening and responsiveness, a practice ensuring the organization hears and values all voices.

Active listening in this context means leaders genuinely engage with the ideas and concerns of their team members, regularly making room for discussions about feelings, fears, and other personal or professional challenges, where the culture views diverse perspectives as essential for innovation. This type of empathetic leadership enhances team dynamics and drives creative solutions.

By responding promptly and thoughtfully to team inputs, leaders reinforce their commitment to everyone's contribution, further solidifying a culture of inclusivity and respect.

A strong stance against workplace bullying is also paramount. When leaders establish clear policies and a zero-tolerance attitude toward bullying, leaders protect their team members from behaviors that undermine team cohesion and individual dignity. This protective measure directly extends from the UNICORN values, particularly empathy and resilience, ensuring that the workplace is safe and supportive for everyone. It also aligns with the responsiveness aspect of UNICORN leadership because leaders must act decisively to resolve conflicts and maintain a healthy workplace.

Through these interconnected practices of active listening, responsiveness, and a firm anti-bullying stance, the workplace transforms into an incubator for innovative ideas energized by diverse perspectives and empathetic leadership. This holistic approach promotes a healthy organizational ecosystem that powers the company forward by leveraging the unique strengths and insights of its people.

THE AUTHENTICITY PARADOX: A CMO'S CONFESSION

Throughout my journey, I've encountered leaders who candidly reveal the stark contrast between their company's marketed culture and the actual internal experience. One revealing conversation was with a Chief Marketing Officer (CMO) who shared a disheartening reality. He confessed, "I know you came to work here based on our 'authenticity videos' and social media posts, but that doesn't apply to us at this level of leadership. Why do you think I'm so boring, and I don't use the perks offered to us? It's because if you do, all people do is gossip and tease and find reasons to dislike you for being different. We may put out videos like that to attract talent, but once you arrive, it's status quo, and that's the rub. That's why people don't last around here for very long. We lie to them coming in the door that we don't require 'sales,' and we lie to them before they even start working here about wanting them to show up as their true, authentic selves. The truth is, those videos are created just to win *Best Workplace* awards."

This candid admission reveals a significant gap between the company's projected image (a Sham Culture, as I call it) and its internal reality, underscoring the superficial adoption of values for external recognition without embedding them into the organizational fabric. Such discrepancies lead to disillusionment (not to mention gaslighting) and high turnover as employees, lured by promises of authenticity and inclusivity, find themselves in environments that stifle their genuine selves and prioritize conformity over diversity.

BRIDGING THE GAP WITH AUTHENTIC LEADERSHIP

For leaders striving to be unicorns in their industry, bridging this authenticity gap is essential. Authentic leadership demands more than marketing slogans; it requires a deep, unwavering commitment to living out these values at every level of the organization.

CREATING A CULTURE OF ACTIVE LISTENING AND RESPONSIVENESS

Consider the tale of a CEO I once worked with, whose predictable "active listening" method involved him leaning back in his chair, sighing in exasperation, turning beet-red in the face, and twirling his glasses. This behavior became a running joke among the team, signaling an impending outburst rather than sincere engagement. This example starkly contrasts with the essence of nurturing a UNICORN-centric culture rooted in genuine commitment to active listening and prompt responsiveness to team members' thoughts and needs.

By adopting a 70-to-30 listening-to-speaking ratio, leaders cultivate an environment rich in open communication and mutual respect. In this framework, leaders value every team member's voice. Leaders who embody and practice this principle unlock the door to inclusivity and innovation, laying the foundation for a thriving team dynamic.

ADDRESSING WORKPLACE BULLYING THROUGH AUTHENTIC LEADERSHIP

This approach to leadership also plays a vital role in addressing and preventing workplace bullying. By establishing an ecosystem where active listening and genuine responsiveness are the norms, leaders ensure all employees can feel safe and respected. This environment discourages behaviors that lead to bullying as team members feel more connected to their leaders, confident that they take their concerns seriously. Leaders who are present and engaged can quickly identify and address bullying, reinforcing a culture of respect and support.

ADDRESSING WORKPLACE BULLYING: A PERSONAL JOURNEY AND BROADER INSIGHTS

As a naturally extroverted individual, I've always been the loudest voice. This vibrancy shouldn't be mistaken for an absence of sensitivity, however. It also doesn't mean I don't need or want respectful feedback. I don't want to be bullied, either.

My first genuine encounter with workplace bullying occurred in this context, as a newly appointed branch manager at a large regional bank in Kansas City, Mo. The district manager, under the guise of using emotional intelligence, publicly criticized those she deemed needing improvement. This wasn't constructive feedback; she wielded a harsh spotlight in team meetings. When I requested more private feedback, her response was dismissive. "Someone as bright and shiny as you should have no problem with public criticism," she said. "Did you think a few tears would change my strategy?"

Despite my professional success, her behavior rocked my confidence. Nearly twenty years later, I still think of her from time to time. And, the truth is, YES. I thought my tears would lead her to adjust her strategy. *How* and *why* would a district manager continue belittling their teammate even after understanding the harm it caused me and the team?

The public nature of the criticism I faced from her exploited my extroverted personality. My former district manager wrongly assumed that my outward confidence shielded me from a painful and public rebuke. This misunderstanding of my character, and the dismissive attitude toward my sincere responses, underscored a critical flaw in the workplace dynamics.

A 2021 Workplace Bullying Institute survey revealed that approximately 61 percent of bullies are bosses, often targeting subordinates who "shine" differently and threaten their sense of control.[1] This experience underscores the urgent need for policies that stress respect and empathy and protect employees from bullying. It's essential to recognize that everyone, regardless of how outwardly vibrant or resilient they may appear, deserves a work environment that respects their dignity and acknowledges their humanity.

GABRIELLE RABON'S NOTABLE NUGGET ON EMPATHY AND UNDERSTANDING IN DIFFICULT CONVERSATIONS

"When a leader acknowledges a misunderstanding or misstep with humility and honesty, it prompts reflection," Gabby says. "What impact did this admission have? Often, such openness leads to deeper discussions among team members, fostering a culture where challenges are addressed head-on. This approach not only resolves immediate issues but also builds lasting trust and safety within the team, essential for preventing workplace bullying."

[1] Gary Namie, "2021 WBI U.S. Workplace Bullying Survey," Workplace Bullying Institute, Retrieved from https://workplacebullying.org/wp-content/uploads/2024/01/2021-Full-Report.pdf .

ENCOURAGING WORK-LIFE INTEGRATION

Rather than clinging to the outdated concept of work-life balance, encouraging work-life integration is a cornerstone of nurturing a UNICORN culture. This approach acknowledges the intertwined nature of personal and professional lives, aiming to create a compassionate and supportive workplace that prioritizes holistic well-being and individual authenticity. Such a shift in perspective cultivates a harmonious environment where employees feel valued, understood, and encouraged to bring their entire selves to work.

However, winning "Best Places to Work" awards sometimes reflect more vanity metrics that appeal to ego-driven leadership than the actual conditions within the organization. These accolades, while flattering, don't translate necessarily into meaningful improvements in workplace culture or employee well-being. They can be a mirage, misleading current employees and potential recruits about the reality of the working environment.

We challenge both employees and UNICORN Leaders to look beyond the company-sponsored narrative. Genuine listening sessions with employees at every level are imperative to uncovering the actual situation and identifying fundamental areas that encourage meaningful engagement and meaningful changes. A mentally healthy employee is more likely to be a mentally sound parent and family member, contributing positively to the broader community.

This understanding underscores the need for organizations to consider roles such as Chief Wellness Officer or on-site licensed clinical professional counselors genuinely dedicated to their teammates' needs. By making these roles integral to their operations, organizations ensure their commitment to holistic well-being isn't just lip service but a tangible, impactful reality that benefits all.

CELEBRATING SUCCESSES AND LEARNING FROM FAILURES

Celebrating successes and openly learning from failures are critical practices for reinforcing a growth mindset within an organization. This approach is not just about recognizing achievements; it's about embracing a cycle of continuous improvement that reflects core UNICORN values.

When organizations celebrate successes, it's essential to highlight how these achievements align with the organization's values. This recognition should go beyond mere acknowledgment and involve specific, actionable insights that others in the organization can learn from and apply. According to a Gallup study, when employees strongly agree they can link their goals to the organization's goals, they are 3.5 times more likely to be engaged.[2] Engaged employees are more likely to embody and champion the organization's vision, mission, and purpose, leading to a more robust and cohesive culture.

When failures occur, organizations shouldn't stigmatize or hide them. They are valuable learning opportunities. A practical method to facilitate this is implementing a "lessons-learned" system where teams share and discuss what didn't work and why without fear of retribution. Research from *Harvard Business Review* confirms that organizations that systematically collect, analyze, and share lessons from failures are more successful at learning from them and adapting.[3]

[2] Denise McLain and Bailey Nelson, "How Effective Feedback Fuels Performance," Gallup, January 1, 2022, https://www.gallup.com/workplace/357764/fast-feedback-fuels-performance.aspx

INNOVATIVE IDEA: THE 'FAILED HEROES' BOARD

To further embed this mindset, consider creating a "Failed Heroes" board or "Innovation Showcase" to highlight innovative and risky ideas that didn't achieve their intended outcomes. This board serves as a testament to the organization's commitment to innovation and learning. By showcasing these "failed" ideas, leaders demonstrate the essential purpose of risk-taking and creative thinking. This practice supports the organization's narrative that celebrates thought leadership and innovation, aligning words with behaviors and encouraging a culture where employees feel safe to experiment.

To further cultivate this culture, organizations can employ specific workplace practices, such as:

- **Regular Retrospectives.** Scheduled meetings where teams reflect on recent projects or periods to discuss what went well and what needs improvement.

- **Recognition Programs.** Tailored to highlight how success at various levels contributes to broader organizational goals, these programs can motivate all employees to strive for excellence and align with core values.

- **Transparency in Decision-Making.** Sharing the rationale behind decisions, especially those that didn't work out as planned, can demystify the process and encourage a more inclusive atmosphere.

[3] Amy C. Edmondson, "Strategies for Learning from Failure," *Harvard Business Review*, last modified April 2011, https://hbr.org/2011/04/strategies-for-learning-from-failure.

By integrating these practices into daily operations, leaders create a growth-centric environment and reinforce their commitment to the values that define an authentic UNICORN culture. These strategies ensure that successes and failures contribute to an ongoing conversation about progress, resilience, and collective learning. A foundation of continuous feedback loops and shared learning solidifies current achievements and sets the stage for implementing additional policies and initiatives that sustain and expand the vision for an inclusive and innovative workplace.

CHAPTER 6

Elevating Visionary UNICORN Leaders for Community and Industry Impact

Never underestimate the importance of weaving strategic and creative practices into daily operations. For example, designing strategic HR policies requires incorporating the diverse needs of your workforce. To be effective, policies should emerge from collaborators, with voices from every job level and demographic within the organization engaged. Such inclusivity leads to comprehensive policies that resonate with practical applications at every organizational level.

COLLABORATIVE POLICY DESIGN:

- **Engage Diverse Stakeholders.** Facilitate workshops or focus groups that include a cross-section of employees to gather a broad range of actionable insights.

- **Leverage Employee Surveys.** Use data from regular surveys to inform policy revisions and address employee needs quickly and effectively.

- **Implement Pilot Programs.** Test new policies in selected departments to refine them based on real-world and real-time feedback.

- **Transparency in Policy Development.** Maintain open communication throughout the policy development process to build trust and ensure inclusivity.

As organizations strategically align policies with UNICORN values, organizations build environments where innovation flourishes and purpose inspires! Such settings are not only compliant with ethical standards (duh!) but also promote a culture where each employee is agile and equipped to meet the challenges of tomorrow.

INNOVATIVE LEADERSHIP PRACTICES

To embody the essence of UNICORN Leadership, organizations must implement practices and clearly communicate expectations that reflect their core values. This affirms a commitment to creating a diverse and forward-thinking workplace where creativity and personal growth are proud priorities.

INNOVATION LABS AND MENTORSHIP PROGRAMS:

- **Innovation Labs.** Use as incubators for new ideas, encouraging cross-functional collaboration and rapid prototyping.

- **Diverse Mentorship Programs.** Pair employees from various ethnic and cultural backgrounds to foster mutual learning and professional growth.

These programs support the UNICORN principles of empathy and inclusivity, enhancing both personal and organizational development.

GLOBAL LEADERSHIP AND CONTINUOUS FEEDBACK

Embracing global leadership programs and continuous feedback mechanisms are critical to creating a UNICORN Culture. These initiatives enable organizations to both adapt to change and drive it, permitting teams to take pleasure in doing so, and promoting a culture of continuous learning and inclusivity:

- **Global Leadership Exchange Programs.** Allow leaders to experience and understand diverse cultural contexts, enhancing global empathy and strategic insights.

- **Continuous Real-Time Feedback Loop.** Establishes a system where feedback is immediate, enabling leaders and team members to adjust their strategies in real-time.

The consistent application of UNICORN values across all organizational layers is essential for cultivating a culture of trust and radical respect. Every teammate feels valued and heard, smoothly bridging any gaps between leadership and the broader team. Leaders who "practice what they preach" validate the trust placed in them by their teams as they model the integrity and authenticity required to create a transformative workplace.

Workplaces and leaders who implement strategic policies and innovative practices aligned with UNICORN values can transform their immediate environments and influence broader societal landscapes. They can pave the way for future generations to inherit a world that values integrity, creativity, and collective well-being.

STRATEGIC ROLE OF CHROS FOR ACTION-ORIENTED CHANGE

Chief Human Resources Officers (CHROs) are crucial in advocating for and actively driving the integration of UNICORN traits—Uniqueness, Nimble-Nurturing, Inspiring, Compassionate, Optimistic, Resilient, and Noble—within the organizational culture. Their leadership is essential in ensuring that diversity, inclusion, and leadership development move from being mere "items on the agenda in order to check a box" to becoming fundamental components of the organization's strategic framework.

NAVIGATING EXECUTIVE PRESSURE

CHROs often face significant pressure from CEOs and boards who demand quick fixes to deep-seated issues. To pursue genuine change, CHROs must recognize and execute within their unique position to advocate for long-term strategies prioritizing ethical leadership and sustainable growth over short-term gains. This involves presenting compelling data and case studies showing the long-term benefits of such an approach, not only for employee satisfaction but for overall organizational resilience and profitability.

IDENTIFYING AND SUPPORTING UNICORN CHROS

Organizations must identify and empower CHROs who embody UNICORN Leader traits. These are leaders who:

- **Challenge the Status Quo.** They fearlessly challenge traditional practices that no longer serve the company well.

- **Lead with Vision.** They see beyond immediate challenges and see what the organization can become by fully embracing diversity and innovation.

- **Foster Inclusive Cultures.** They implement policies and practices that value all voices, driving deeper engagement and creativity across the organization.

ACTION STEPS FOR CHROS:

1. **Develop and Communicate Clear Objectives.** Define what diversity, inclusion, and leadership development look like within the organization. *Create measurable goals and regular reporting metrics* for the CEO and board.

2. **Implement Comprehensive Training Programs.** Focus on developing the skills related to UNICORN traits, such as empathy, resilience, and ethical decision-making for leaders at all levels.

3. **Create a Feedback Loop.** Establish channels for continuous feedback on diversity and inclusion efforts, using this input to make data-driven adjustments to HR policies and initiatives.

4. **Champion Employee Resource Groups (ERGs).** Support and provide resources for ERGs that align with diverse identities and experiences, using these groups as a springboard for broader cultural shifts within the organization.

ENGAGING THE BOARD

CHROs should work closely with the board to ensure that the strategic importance of UNICORN Leader traits are recognized at the highest level. This includes:

- **Educational Sessions.** Regular sessions with the board about the latest trends in HR and the proven benefits of a diverse and inclusive workplace.

- **Strategic HR Planning.** Including HR objectives in the organization's strategic plan ensures they're prioritized and that resources are on par with financial and operational goals.

By taking these actions, CHROs position themselves to respond to the immediate demands of their roles. They also redefine what it means to lead Human Resources authentically and prepare their organizations for future peaks and valleys.

INTEGRATING UNICORN LEADERSHIP FOR MULTI-GENERATIONAL WORKPLACE HARMONY

As business landscapes change, the traits of UNICORN Leaders—Uniqueness, Nimble-Nurturing, Inspiring, Compassionate, Optimistic, Resilient, and Noble—increasingly influence the success and sustainability of workplaces worldwide. These traits help organizations manage the complexities of a multi-generational workforce. Leveraging the diverse perspectives and skills of various age groups undergirds a cohesive and innovative environment.

Effective UNICORN Leaders can bridge generational gaps by promoting an understanding, nimble-nurturing, and inclusive culture. These approaches enhance team cohesion and fuel collective innovation by amplifying the strengths inherent in each generation. For instance, combining the fresh, tech-savvy insights of younger employees with the seasoned strategies of older colleagues can lead to groundbreaking innovations and solutions that might not emerge in a more homogenized team.

To further enhance your ability to lead such diverse workplaces effectively and future-proof your leadership skills, it's beneficial to engage with a variety of resources. These include contemporary leadership courses, workshops focused on diversity and inclusion, and publications that explore the intersection of generational dynamics and leadership practices. Engaging with these resources will deepen your understanding of effective multi-generational management. They will also equip you to implement UNICORN traits more effectively within your organization.

RESOURCES FOR FUTURE-PROOF LEADERSHIP

To equip yourself with the tools to lead effectively in a changing business world, consider engaging with the following resources:

THE *UNICORN LEADER IMPACT ASSESSMENT*

The *UNICORN Leader Impact Assessment* helps you evaluate and enhance various aspects of your leadership style, from decision-making and team engagement to resilience and ethical practice. This potent resource helps leaders refine their approach and ensure their methods are resilient, innovative, and adaptable to future challenges.

WHY ENGAGE WITH THE *UNICORN LEADER IMPACT ASSESSMENT?*

- **Targeted Insight.** Gain a deeper understanding of how your leadership affects your team and organization, with specific focus areas that align with modern challenges.

- **Actionable Feedback.** Receive detailed feedback on your leadership strengths and areas for improvement. This will help you construct a focused development plan.

- **Strategic Development.** Use the insights and strategies derived from the assessment to craft a leadership style that anticipates the needs of your workplace and industry.

DON'T MISS OUR OFFER

After completing the assessment, you receive an offer to book a personalized consultation with Lighthouse Leadership Consultants. This session will tailor a strategic plan based on your unique results, enabling you to apply UNICORN leadership principles more effectively within your organization.

This resource isn't just about learning where you stand today. It prepares you for tomorrow's leadership challenges. By engaging with the UNICORN Leader Impact Assessment, you commit to a journey of continuous growth and innovation that will define your legacy as a next-level leader.

HARVARD BUSINESS REVIEW'S 'MANAGING PEOPLE FROM 5 GENERATIONS' GUIDE

The *Harvard Business Review*'s "Managing People from 5 Generations Guide"[1] offers valuable insights into effectively managing generational diversity in the workplace. It provides strategies and tips on how to meet the different needs and motivations of each generation, promoting a more effective and harmonious working environment.

Both resources equip you to excel in leading a diverse workforce, ensuring that every team member, regardless of age, feels valued and understood. Take these steps today to empower your leadership and workplaces, and prepare for the next generation of Unicorn Leaders.

---

[1] Rebecca Knight, "Managing People from 5 Generations," *Harvard Business Review*, last modified September 25, 2014, https://hbr.org/2014/09/managing-people-from-5-generations

CHAPTER 7

Be the Change:
Rise of the UNICORN Leader

This playbook dives into the depths of UNICORN Leadership, a transformative force that redefines success in the modern workplace and propels us toward a prosperous future with innovation, empathy, and justice. As we reach the last pages, remember that becoming a UNICORN Leader reaches beyond embodying traits to spearheading a movement that promotes a fairer, more innovative, and compassionate world.

We sincerely thank our readers for embarking on this journey with us. Your dedication to exploring and practicing these principles ignite our collective mission to transform leadership norms. To the inspiring UNICORN Leaders who shared their wisdom and trailblazing leadership paths—your stories and successes light the way for others to follow.

The time for change is now. Lighthouse Leadership Consultants can partner with you during this transformative journey. We're not just observers; we facilitate change. We designed our services—from delivering powerful keynotes that inspire thousands to hosting workshops that galvanize teams around new ideas—to challenge the status quo and catalyze meaningful change. When we partner with you, we pledge to influence outcomes, impact bottom lines, and use our leadership strengths for the greater good.

JOIN THE STAMPEDE!

Visit LighthouseLeadershipConsultants.com to learn how we can help your organization embrace and implement UNICORN principles. Connect with like-minded leaders, discover resources that support your growth, and engage with a community committed to making a difference. Whether you want to inspire your team, enhance your organizational culture, or lead with a transformative impact, we are here to assist you.

Together, we can smash boundaries and develop UNICORN Leaders who leave a lasting, positive imprint on our world. Join us and be part of a movement that isn't only about leading but about transforming the concept of leadership itself.

This is our time. This is our movement. The future of leadership is here—and it starts with you, dear UNICORN Leader.

UNLOCK YOUR LEADERSHIP POTENTIAL WITH THE *UNICORN LEADER IMPACT ASSESSMENT*

Are you ready to truly understand and amplify your leadership impact? We are excited to introduce the *Unicorn Leader Impact Assessment*, your next pivotal step toward becoming a UNICORN Leader.

WHY ENGAGE WITH THE *UNICORN LEADER IMPACT ASSESSMENT?*

This isn't just another assessment. It's a gateway to a deeper understanding of how your leadership style resonates within your organization and beyond. Through a detailed evaluation, you will discover how to drive impact and influence effectively in the modern workplace. Whether you're looking to enhance your strategic insights or foster a culture of innovation and resilience, we designed this assessment with actionable insights tailored to your unique leadership journey. These are the benefits:

- **Deep Drill into Your Leadership Dynamics.** Understand the nuances of your leadership style and how it influences your team and organizational outcomes.

- **Receive Feedback for Strategic Growth.** Enhance your specific leadership traits and address your unique challenges with personalized feedback.

- **Empower Your Leadership Transformation.** With each aspect of the assessment, you will gain insights that highlight your strengths and pinpoint areas for development, ensuring your growth trajectory is both impactful and sustainable.

TAKE THE FIRST STEP TODAY

Don't wait! Unlock your full potential. **Visit Lighthouse Leadership Consultants** to access the Unicorn Leader Impact Assessment now. Complete the assessment today to start your journey toward becoming a visionary leader who leads with purpose and a profound impact.

Embrace the opportunity to transform your leadership and organizational culture. Engage with the Unicorn Leader Impact Assessment and watch as you and your team amplify your impact, paving the way for future-proof success.

COMING SOON: GO BEHIND THE SCENES WITH *C-SUITE UNICORN*

If you've enjoyed the insights and strategies in *UNICORN Leader: Driving Innovation and Influence in the Modern Workplace*, get ready for the upcoming release of my next book, *C-Suite Unicorn*. While this playbook arms you with a toolkit for transformative leadership, *C-Suite Unicorn* promises an insider's view of the corporate world with less filter and more flair.

C-Suite Unicorn isn't your typical leadership manual. Candid and authentic, this manual addresses the realities of navigating the highs and lows of corporate leadership. Where *UNICORN Leader* provides the polished tools and frameworks for leadership excellence, C-Suite Unicorn shares the unvarnished truths and personal anecdotes from my journey and those of fellow leaders who've dared to transform the corporate landscape.

Expect tales that are as instructive as they are entertaining, filled with the nitty-gritty details of boardroom battles, strategic gambits, and the personal challenges that define the path to executive leadership. This book will reveal the soap opera behind the success stories, showing you the raw, unfiltered challenges that leaders face and how they overcome them with resilience, creativity, and, of course, a touch of unicorn magic.

WHY SHOULD YOU READ *C-SUITE UNICORN?*

- **To Get Real.** Discover the less-polished side of leadership, where challenges lurk behind every decision.

- **To Be Inspired.** Learn from the bold moves and brave hearts of those who have navigated the stormy waters of top-tier leadership.

- **To Prepare Yourself.** Equip yourself with the insights that only come from genuine experiences of those at the helm of change.

Stay tuned for the release of *C-Suite Unicorn*, and prepare to delve deeper into the transformative and tumultuous world of leadership. Join me as we strip away the facade and get down to the business of making real, impactful change in the corporate world.

MEET THE UNICORN LEADERS

KRISTI STRAW

Kristi Straw is a trailblazing leader with a rich legacy of shaping the future of Fortune 500 companies. As the founder of Lighthouse Leadership Consultants, she pioneered the INSIGHT Method, revolutionizing change leadership and organizational transformation. Known for her dynamic approach and heart-centered leadership, Kristi empowers leaders to embrace innovation and authenticity. Her extensive experience and vivid vision make her a standout figure in modern leadership. In *UNICORN Leader: Driving Innovation and Influence in the Modern Workplace*, Kristi shares her insights on leading with purpose and influence, offering a comprehensive guide to future-proofing workplaces and leadership.

On a personal note, Kristi is married to Michael Straw, a licensed mental health therapist and the Chief Wellness Officer at Lighthouse Leadership Consultants. They met while attending Eastern Illinois University and have three children, Kingston, Sophia, and Isabella, along with their hunting dog, Remi. The family enjoys traveling and cheering on their children in football, volleyball, and softball games, enriching Kristi's approach to leadership with a deeply empathetic and balanced perspective.

ROBIN SPEAKS, JR.

Robin "R.J." Speaks, Jr. is a Vice President at First Horizon Corporation. Before joining First Horizon in 2023, R.J. was a regional executive at Bank OZK, with previous roles at Branch Banking and Trust and SunTrust Bank. An active community member, he serves on the YMCA board, Smart Start, Junior Achievers, Rotary Club, and the Yadkin County Umpire Association. R.J. holds a Bachelor of Arts degree in financial planning and small business management from Catawba College. His chapter in *UNICORN Leader: Driving Innovation and Influence in the Modern Workplace* explores the intersection of noble and ethical leadership within the financial services sector.

DR. DIEDRICK GRAHAM

Dr. Diedrick Graham is the vice president for culture and strategy at The Healy+ Group. With extensive experience in DEI, organizational development, and conflict resolution, he has served in prominent roles at Princeton University, San Diego State University, and the University of Kansas. As a certified trainer, lecturer, and coach, Dr. Graham's work is pivotal in promoting diversity, equity, and inclusion across various sectors. In *UNICORN Leader: Driving Innovation* and Influence in the Modern Workplace, his insights guide leaders in navigating complex workplace issues to create more inclusive environments.

VINEET MAGO

Vineet "Vinny" Mago is an award-winning and internationally cited leader known for his expertise in sales, training, education, and DEI initiatives. With a diverse background in television, telecom, construction, financial services, and the nonprofit sector, Vinny is dedicated to executive coaching and hosting breakthrough sessions. A proud Florida State University alumnus, he enjoys rock climbing, endurance cycling, and planning adventures with his wife, Sarah, and dog, Matilda. In *UNICORN Leader: Driving Innovation and Influence in the Modern Workplace*, Vinny shares his passion for leadership and his philosophy of being the change you wish to see in the world.

GABRIELLE RABON

Gabrielle "Gabby" Rabon brings her extensive 24-year background in banking and technology to enrich "UNICORN Leader." A seasoned expert in branch banking, strategic partnerships, and leadership, Gabby has woven her deep insights into every page. In *UNICORN Leader: Driving Innovation and Influence in the Modern Workplace*, her experiences, featured in engaging callout boxes, highlight transformative strategies in leadership and workplace dynamics. Gabby's journey as a UNICORN Leader has flourished under Kristi's guidance, embodying the book's principles of growth and innovation.

References

Briggs Myers, Isabel, and Peter B. Meyers. 1995. *Gifts Differing: Understanding Personality Type*. First Edition ed. Mountain View, California: Davies-Black Publishing.

Brown, Brené. 2018. *Dare to Lead: Brave Work.Tough Conversations. Whole Hearts*. New York, United States: Random House.

Edmondson, Amy C. 2011. "Strategies for Learning from Failure." In *Harvard Business Review*. Strategies for Learning from Failure. https://hbr.org/2011/04/strategies-for-learning-from-failure.

Hess, Jared, dir. 2004. *Napoleon Dynamite*. United States: Fox Searchlight Pictures, Paramount Pictures, MTV Films.

King Jr., Dr. Martin L. 2024. "The King Philosophy - Nonviolence365®." The King Center. https://tinyurl.com/u7stkvzt.

Knight, Rebecca. 2014. "Managing People from 5 Generations." *Harvard Business Review*. https://hbr.org/2014/09/managing-people-from-5-generations.

McLain, Denise, and Bailey Nelson. 2024. "How Effective Feedback Fuels Performance." Gallup. https://www.gallup.com/workplace/357764/fast-feedback-fuels-performance.aspx.

Namie, Gary. 2021. *2021 WBI U.S. Workplace Bullying Survey*. https://workplacebullying. org/wp-content/uploads/2024/01/2021-Full-Report.pdf.

Rosenberg, Marshall B. 2003. *Nonviolent Communication: A Language of Life*. 2nd ed. Encinitas, California: PuddleDancer Press.

Schneider, Bruce D. 2022. *Energy Leadership: The 7 Level Framework for Mastery In Life and Business*. N.p.: Wiley.

Scott, Kim. 2019. *Radical Candor: Fully Revised & Updated Edition: Be A Kick-Ass Boss Without Losing Your Humanity*. London, United Kingdom: Pan Books.

Smith, J. 2020. "The Role of Compassion in High-Pressure Industries." In *Harvard Business Review*. N.p.: Harvard Business Publishing. https://hbr.org/.

Printed in Dunstable, United Kingdom

65995701R00060